FOR MOTHER: A BOUQUET OF SENTIMENTS

Great Quotations Publishing Company

0 43422 69512 6

Compiled by: Debbie Hansen
Cover Art by: Joanne Fink
Cover Design by: Jeff Maniglia
Typeset and Design by: Caroline Solarski and
Julie Otlewis

—•—

©1995 Great Quotations Publishing Company

Published by Great Quotations Publishing Company
1967 Quincy Court
Glendale Heights, Illinois 60139

ISBN: 1-56245-073-5

Printed in Hong Kong

The more a child becomes aware
of a mother's willingness to listen,
the more a mother will begin to hear.

A family is a unit composed not only of children,
but of fathers, mothers, an occasional animal
and at times, the common cold.

— Ogden Nash

A young branch takes on all the bends
that one gives to it.

— Chinese Proverb

It is truly wonderful to see what an effect
being much in the air has upon this child;
she is always a merry creature,
but when she is much out of doors
she seems to be almost crazy with happiness.

— Mary Wordsworth

As I watch her at play...
it came to me that this child would pass through life
as the angels live in heaven.

—Pearl Buck

Spinach:
Divide into little piles.
Rearrange again into new piles.
After five or six maneuvers,
sit back and say you are full.

— Delia Ephron

Who takes the child by the hand, takes the mother by the heart.

— Danish Proverb

When a girl hits thirteen,
you can just watch her lose her mind.
Luckily, she gets it back;
but during the time that it's misplaced,
you can lose your own.

A child should be loved for who she is,
not for what she does.

I do not teach children,
I give them joy.

— Isadora Duncan

No time to marry, no time to settle down;
I'm a young woman,
and I ain't done runnin' around.

— Bessie Smith

Take a walk together with your children.
Just talk about the "stuff" of their lives.

All that I am or hope to be,
I owe to my mother.

— Attributed to Lincoln

A mother is...
A parent who remains sane
only because she never knows
what her three-year-old is going to do next.

— Evan Esar

God could not be everywhere,
so therefore he made mothers.

— Hebrew Proverb

You have three names.
The name you inherit,
the name your parents gave you,
and the name you make for yourself.

Parents of teens and parents of babies
have something in common.
They spend a great deal of time
trying to get their kids to talk.

—Paul Swets

When we see great men and women, we give credit to their mothers.

— Charlotte Perkins Gilman

◖◗

We should measure affection,
not by the ardor of its passion,
but by its strength and constancy.

—Cicero

◖◗

No matter how old a mother is
she watches her middle-aged children
for signs of improvement.

— Florida Scott-Maxwell

We cannot put mothering into a formula
and come up with a person
who has the special feeling for your child
that you do.

— Dr. Sally E. Shaywitz

L̶evel with your child by being honest.
Nobody spots a phony
quicker than a child.

— M. MacCracken

Dear Mother —
You know that nothing can ever change
what we have always been
and will always be to each other.

— Franklin Roosevelt

Mother:
The person who *sits* up with you
when you are sick,
and *puts* up with you
when you are well.

There is no friendship, no love,
like that of the mother for the child.

— Henry Ward Beecher

Who ran to help me when I fell,
And would some pretty story tell,
Or kiss the place to make it well?
My Mother.

—Anne Taylor

Reasoning with a child is fine,
if you can reach the child's reason
without destroying your own.

— John Mason Brown

Parents must get across the idea that,
"I love you always,
but sometimes I do not love
your behavior."

— Amy Vanderbilt

I never understood the obstacles
my mother faced,
until I became one.
I love my mother's memory
now more than ever.

Other things may change us,
but we start and end with the family.

— Anthony Brandt

Love children especially...
they live to soften and purify our hearts.
Woe to him who offends a child.

— Feodor Dostoevsky

The best gift a mother can give her child
is the gift of herself.

Mothers are the most unselfish,
the most responsible people in the world.

— Bernard M. Baruch

Where can one better be
than the bosom of one's own family.

A parent is embarrassed
when her child tells a lie,
and even more embarrassed
when he tells the truth.

— Evan Esar

For the hand that rocks the cradle
is the hand that rules the world.

— William Ross Wallace

Children who despise their parents
do so until about age forty,
when they suddenly become like them.

You can multiply all the relations of life,
have more than one sister or brother;
in the course of events,
have more than one wife,
but you never can have but one mother!

If it is desirable that children be kind,
appreciative, and pleasant,
then those qualities should be taught —
not hoped for.

There is only one pretty child in the world,
and every mother has it.

— English Proverb

Perhaps nobody becomes more competent
in hitting a moving target
than a mother spoon feeding a baby.

It was when I had my first child
that I understood
how much my mother loved me.

Before I got married
I had six theories about bringing up children;
now I have six children
and no theories.

She is just an extraordinary mother
and a gentle person.
I depended on her for everything...
I watched her become a strong person,
and that had an enormous influence on me.

— Rosalynn Carter

A child's hand in yours —
what tenderness and power it arouses.
You are instantly the very touchstone
of wisdom and strength.

— Marjorie Holms

Rejecting things
because they are old-fashioned
would rule out the sun and the moon —
and a mother's love.

A mother's heart
is a baby's most beautiful dwelling.

— Ed Dussault

Babies are such a nice way to start people.

Children are the anchors
that hold a mother to life.

—Sophocles

Truth, which is important to a scholar,
has got to be concrete.
And there's nothing more concrete
than dealing with babies,
burps, bottles and frogs.

— Jeane Kirkpatrick

Nothing else will ever make you as happy or as sad,
as proud or as tired, as motherhood.

— Elia Parsons

If evolution really works,
how come mothers have only two hands?

— Ed Dussault

In motherhood there's so much to learn,
so much to give,
and although the learning gets less with each child,
the giving never does.

— Marguerite Kelly

My mother had a great deal of trouble with me,
but I think she enjoyed it.

— Mark Twain

You don't choose your family.
They are God's gift to you,
as you are to them.

— Desmond Tutu

Who is getting more pleasure from this rocking,
the baby or me?

— Nancy Thayer

A baby enters your home
and makes so much noise
for twenty years you can hardly stand it —
then departs, leaving the house so silent
you think you'll go mad.

— Dr. J. A. Holmes

An important thing for parents
to teach their children
is how to get along without them.

— F. Clark

Be kind to thy mother,
for when thou were young,
who loved thee so fondly as she?

— Margaret Courtney

A mother's love is patient and forgiving
when all others are forsaking,
and it never fails or falters,
even though the heart is breaking.

— Helen Steiner Rice

༺C ༄༅༽

Somehow, when you're a child,
you simply accept each turn of events as it comes,
as if there is no other way
for the world to be.

— Isabel Huggan

One mother is worth more
than one hundred school masters.

Remember, when your child has a tantrum, don't have one of your own.

— Dr. J. Kuriansky

The imprint of the mother remains forever
on the life of the child.

Children miss nothing in sizing up their parents.
If you are only half convinced of your beliefs,
they will quickly discern that fact.

— James Dobson

A mother should be like a quilt —
keep the children warm
but don't smother them.

Give a little love to a child
and you get a great deal back.

— John Ruskin

You can be sure it's her first-born
if a mother cries
when her youngster starts school.

A mother's patience
is like a tube of toothpaste —
it's never quite gone.

Parents learn a lot from their children
about coping with life.

— Muriel Spark

A mother is not a person to lean on
but a person to make leaning unnecessary.

— Dorothy Fischer

The joys of mothers and fathers are secret,
and so are their griefs and fears.

— Francis Bacon

A man loves his sweetheart the most,
his wife the best,
but his mother the longest.

— Irish Proverb

Allow children to be happy their own way;
for what better way will they ever find?

— Dr. Samuel Johnson

Life is the first gift,
love is the second,
and understanding the third.

I love being a mother.
I am more aware.
I feel things on a deeper level.
I have a kind of understanding about my body,
about being a woman.

— Shelley Long

A woman who can cope
with the terrible twos
can cope with anything.

Loving a child doesn't mean
giving in to all his whims;
to love him is to bring out the best in him,
to teach him to love what is difficult.

— Nadia Boulanger

There is no influence so powerful
as that of the mother.

— Sarah Josepha Hale

When you are a mother,
you are never really alone in your thoughts.
You are connected to your child
and to all those who touch your lives.
A mother always has to think twice,
once for herself
and once for her child.

— Sophia Loren

$\langle\!\langle \odot \, \odot \rangle\!\rangle$

All the earth,
though it were full of kind hearts,
is but a desolation
and deserted place to a mother
when her only child is absent.

— Elizabeth Gaskell

Never help a child with a task
at which he feels he can succeed.

— M. Montessori

We never know the love of the parent
until we become parents ourselves.

— Henry Ward Beecher

Small children can disturb your sleep,
big children your life.

— Yiddish Proverb

If you want your child to accept your values
when he reaches his teen years,
then you must be worthy of his respect
during his younger days.

— James Dobson

$\text{\scriptsize ❧ ❧}$

Being a mother, as far as I can tell,
is a constantly evolving process of adapting
to the needs of your child
while also changing and growing
as a person in your own right.

— Deborah Insel

A wonderful motto for teens and parents
is to never needlessly harm
the respect of another.

— Dr. Kay Kuzma

The mother is the medium
which the primitive infant transforms
into a socialized human being.

— Beata Rank

The character and history of each child
may be a new and poetic experience to the parent,
if he will let it.

— Margaret Fuller

Making terms with reality,
with things as they are,
is a full time business for the child.

— Milton Sapirstein

A little child, a limber self.
Singing, dancing to itself...
Makes such a vision to the sight,
as fills a mother's eyes with light.

One of the closest bonds
a mother can have with her daughter
comes through comforting.

Any mother could perform the jobs
of several air traffic controllers with ease.

— Lisa Alther

Were women meant to do everything —
work *and* have babies?

— Candice Bergen

The mother is the most precious possession
of the nation,
so precious that society advances
its highest well-being
when it protects the functions of the mother.

—Ellen Key

If motherhood is an occupation
which is critically important
to society the way we say it is,
then there should be a mother's bill of rights.

— Barbara Ann Mikulski

Our children are not going to be
just "our children" —
they are going to be
other people's husbands and wives
and the parents of our grandchildren.

— Mary S. Calderone

...some day you will be old enough
to start reading fairy tales again.

—C. S. Lewis

What a mother says to her children
is not heard by the world,
but it will be heard by posterity.

The trouble with being a parent
is that by the time you're experienced
you're unemployable.

—H. Less

Let your children go
if you want to keep them.

—M. Forbes

Children are likely to live up to
what you believe of them.

— Lady Bird Johnson

‹‹© ©››

It's not flesh and blood,
but the heart
that makes us mothers and daughters.

‹‹© ©››

When I stopped seeing my mother
with the eyes of a child,
I saw the woman who helped me
give birth to myself.

— Nancy Friday

Everyone knows a great deal
about one child — herself.

My first job is to be a good mother.

— Faye Dunaway

Most mothers are instinctive philosophers.

— Harriet Beecher Stowe

Part of the good part of being a parent
is a constant sense of déjà vu.
But some of what you have to *vu*
you never want to *vu* again.

— Anna Quindlen

Cleaning your house
while your kids are still growing
is like shoveling the walk
before it stops snowing.

— Phyllis Diller

My mother wanted me to be her wings,
to fly as she never quite had the courage to do.
I love her for that.
I love that she wanted to give birth
to her own wings.

— Erica Jong

A mother is not a person to lean on
but a person to make leaning unnecessary.

— Dorothy Canfield Fisher

A mother is neither cocky, nor proud,
because she knows
the school principle may call at any minute
to report that her child
has just driven a motorcycle
through the gymnasium.

— Mary Kay Blakely

There is a point
where you aren't as much parents and children
as you are adults and friends.

— Jamie Lee Curtis

The ultimate test of relationship
is not to disagree
but to hold hands.

— Alexandra Penny

I was not a classic mother.
But my kids were never palmed off
to boarding school.
So I didn't bake cookies.
You can buy cookies,
but you can't buy love.

— Raquel Welch

Loving a child is a circular business.
The more you give, the more you get,
the more you want to give.

— Penelope Leach

I began to love this little creature
and to anticipate his birth
as a fresh twist to a knot,
which I do not wish to untie.

— Mary Wollstonecraft

（◖ ◗）

What a distressing contrast there is
between the radiant intelligence of the child
and the feeble mentality of the average adult.

—S. Freud

Life is the first gift,
love the second
and understanding the third.

— Marge Piercy

◖◗

Parents of young children should realize
that few people,
and maybe no one,
will find their children
as enchanting as they do.

— Barbara Walters

When a child enters the world through you,
it alters everything on a psychic,
psychological and purely practical level.

— Jane Fonda

The darn trouble with cleaning the house
is it gets dirty the next day anyway,
so skip a week if you have to.
The children are the most important thing.

— Barbara Bush

The most important thing
a mother can do for her children
is to love their father.

Seeing you sleeping peacefully on your back
among your stuffed ducks, bears and basset hounds
would remind me
that no matter how good the next day might be,
certain moments were gone forever.

— Joan Baez

If youth is a defect,
it is one we outgrow too soon.

— Robert Lowell

The father is the head of the house —
the mother is the heart of the house.

An infallible way to make your child miserable
is to satisfy all his demands.

Necessity is the mother
of taking chances.

—Mark Twain

I stood in the hospital corridor
the night after she was born.
Through a window I could see
all the small, crying newborn infants
and somewhere among them
slept the one who was mine.
I stood there for hours filled with happiness
until the night nurse sent me to bed.

— Liv Ullman

I looked on child rearing
not only as a work of love and duty
but as a profession
that was fully as interesting and challenging
as any honorable profession in the world
and one that demanded
the best that I could bring to it.

— Rose Kennedy

No one had told her what it would be like,
the way she loved her children.
What a thing of the body it was,
as physically rooted as sexual desire,
but without its edge of danger.

— Mary Gordon

While you can quarrel with a grown-up,
how can you quarrel with a newborn baby
who has stretched out his little arms
for you to pick him up?

— Maria Von Trapp

I actually remember feeling delight,
at two o'clock in the morning,
when the baby woke for his feed,
because I so longed to have another look at him.

— Margaret Drabble

In the sheltered simplicity of the first days
after a baby is born,
one sees again the magical closed circle,
the miraculous sense of two people
existing only for each other.

— Anne Morrow Lindbergh

There must always be a struggle
between a mother and a daughter,
while one aims at power
the other at independence.

The walks and talks we have
with our two-year-olds in red boots
have a great deal to do with the values
they will cherish as adults.

— Edith F. Hunter

Little children are still the symbol
of the eternal marriage
between love and duty.

— George Eliot

It will be gone before you know it.
The fingerprints on the wall
appear higher and higher.
Then suddenly they disappear.

We are together, my child and I.
Mother and child, yes, but sisters really,
against whatever denies us all that we are.

— Alice Walker

Women as the guardians of children
possess great power.
They are the molders of their children's personalities
and the arbiters of their development.

— Ann Oakley

Praise your children openly,
reprove them secretly.

—W. Cecil

$\mathbf{D}$o not, on a rainy day,
ask your child what he feels like doing,
because I assure you
that what he feels like doing,
you won't feel like watching.

— Fran Lebowitz

You can do anything with children
if you only play with them.

I have found the happiness of parenthood
greater than any other that I have experienced.

The phrase "working mother" is redundant.

— Jane Sellman

There is so much to teach,
and the time goes so fast.

— Erma Bombeck

Your children are always your "babies",
even if they have gray hair.

— Janet Leigh

In bringing up children,
what good mothers and fathers
instinctively feel like doing for their babies
is usually best after all.

— Benjamin Spock

Ify ou want a baby,
have a new one.
Don't baby the old one.

— Jessamyn West

A torn jacket is soon mended;
but hard words bruise the heart of a child.

— Henry Wadsworth Longfellow

Train your child in the way
in which you know
you should have gone yourself.

— C. H. Spurgeon

W ords which explode
at an impressionable moment
in the life of a young child,
can shape an entire personality.

— Gordon MacDonald

Children are a great comfort in your old age.
And they help you reach it sooner too.

— Lionel M. Kauffman

When you are dealing with a child,
keep all your wits about you,
and sit on the floor.

— A. O'Malley

The third baby is the easiest...
You know, for instance,
how you're going to look in a maternity dress
about the seventh month,
and you know how to release the footbrake
on a baby carriage without fumbling amateurishly.

— Shirley Jackson

There is nothing more thrilling
in this world,
I think,
than having a child that is yours,
and yet is mysteriously a stranger.

— Agatha Christie

I do not love him because he is good,
but because he is my little child.

Mommy herself has told us
that she looked upon us more as her friends
than her daughters.
Now that is all very fine,
but still, a friend can't take a mother's place.
I need my mother as an example which I can follow,
I want to be able to respect her.

— Anne Frank

H appy is he that is happy in his children.

— Thomas Fuller

There's a lot more to being a woman
than being a mother,
but there's a hell of a lot more to being a mother
than most people suspect.

— Roseanne Barr

Our children immediately discern the gap between what we *say* and what we *do*.

Children are our most valuable resource.

— Herbert Hoover

Children are true connoisseurs.
What's precious to them has no price —
only value.

— Bel Kaufman

Children are such sticky things,
'specially after tea.

— E. F. Benson

Give love to a little child,
and you get a great deal back.

— John Ruskin

OTHER TITLES BY GREAT QUOTATIONS

201 Best Things Ever Said
A Lifetime of Love
A Light Heart Lives Long
A Teacher Is Better Than Two Books
The ABC's of Parenting
As A Cat Thinketh
The Best of Friends
The Birthday Astrologer
Cheatnotes On Life
Chicken Soup
Don't Deliberate . . . Litigate
Fantastic Father, Dependable Dad
For Mother—A Bouquet of Sentiments
Global Wisdom
Golden Years, Golden Words
Growing Up In TOYLAND
Happiness Is Found Along The Way
Heal The World
Hollywords
Hooked on Golf
I'm Not Over The Hill
In Celebration of Women
Inspirations

Interior Design For Idiots
Let's Talk Decorating
Life's Simple Pleasures
Money For Nothing, Tips For Free
Motivating Quotes For Motivated People
Mrs. Aesop's Fables
Mrs. Murphy's Laws
Mrs. Webster's Dictionary
Mrs. Webster's Guide To Business
Parenting 101
Real Estate Agents and Their
   Dirty Little Tricks
Reflections
Romantic Rhapsody
The Secret Language of Men
The Secret Language of Women
The Sports Page
Some Things Never Change
TeenAge Of Insanity
Thanks From The Heart
Things You'll Learn, If You Live
   Long Enough
Women On Men

GREAT QUOTATIONS PUBLISHING COMPANY

1967 Quincy Court
Glendale Heights, IL 60139-2045
Phone (708) 582-2800
Fax (708) 582-2813